A BOOK ALL ABOUT

OUR PRECIOUS POOPER

A Brutally Honest Journal of Baby's First Few Years

by Megan Rubiner Zinn

KNOCK KNOCK
VENICE, CALIFORNIA

Created, published, and distributed by Knock Knock
1635-B Electric Ave.
Venice, CA 90291
knockknockstuff.com
Knock Knock is a registered trademark of Knock Knock LLC

Illustrations by Rachel Katstaller

ISBN: 978-160106831-6
UPC: 825703-50224-4

10 9 8 7 6 5 4 3 2

TABLE OF CONTENTS

INTRODUCTION

Did your parents lovingly record the first time you threw your poop across the room or the first time you bolted in a crowded grocery store? Probably not. They recorded the typical milestones: your first smile, your first steps, and your first haircut—and overlooked all of the memorable stuff. Those milestones are important, sure, but your baby also does all sorts of funny, annoying, infuriating, disgusting, and completely inexplicable things.

That's where *Our Precious Pooper* comes in. Record the ridiculous stuff here, including sketches, diagrams, maps, incriminating photos, perhaps even smears of body fluids

if you feel it's important. In a few years, when the PTSD wears off, you'll be able to look back and laugh at, or at least acknowledge, the fact that you survived with your sanity intact. After that, *Our Precious Pooper* will serve as an ideal tool for embarrassing your child, especially during the teenage years.

Having a child doesn't make your life perfect, and it doesn't mean it's over, either. It will just be a lot weirder. A lot. Make sure you keep track of all that weirdness.

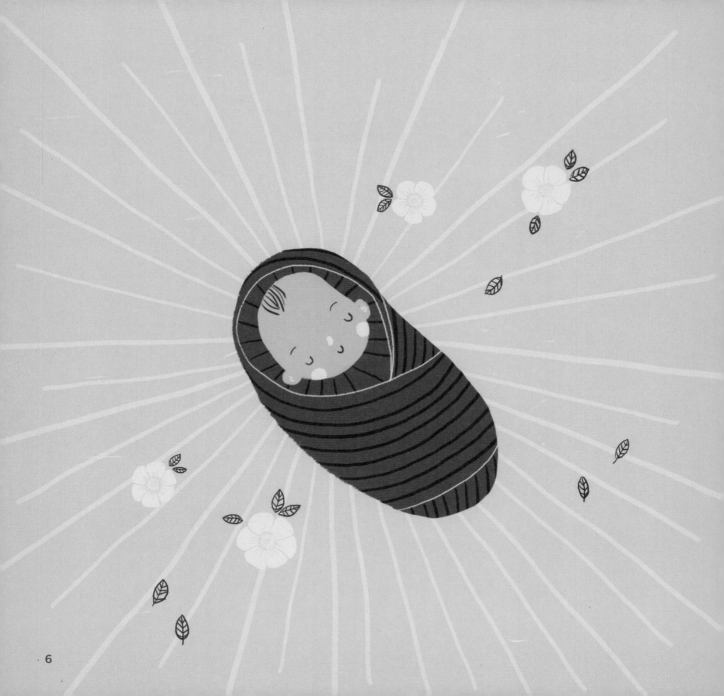

JUST THE FACTS

A CURSORY LIST OF BASIC STATS

Name: _____

Date of birth: _____

Time of day: _____

Height: _____

Weight: _____

Apgar score: _____

Identifying marks: _____

_____

Family members present at the birth: _____

_____

Midwife, doctor, doula, nurses present: _____

_____

Weather: _____

_____

Days past (or before) due date: _____

ATTACH BABY'S
PHOTO HERE

HOW WE GOT HERE IN THE FIRST PLACE

CONCEPTION, PREGNANCY, PLANNING

In the olden days, there was really only one way to get pregnant, whether it was on a honeymoon in Niagara Falls or in the back seat of a Buick. These days, you might get pregnant the old-fashioned way—or in a doctor's office, inside a petri dish, or with the help of a surrogate or an adoption agency. If you're the pregnant one, it's a wild nine months, during which your body will surprise you and freak you out and you'll finally master peeing in a cup without getting it on your hands.

Was the pregnancy planned? Don't lie. _____

_____

Where did you get pregnant?

_____

_____

_____

The fantasy of constant unprotected sex became a nightmare after

_____ days/weeks. *(circle one)*

The thrill of pregnancy wore off on

_____. *(date)*

Strangest food(s) you craved:

_____

_____

_____

Most hideous morning sickness experience: _____

_____

_____

You ate _____ just before barfing
and will therefore never eat it again.

Delicious banned foods you missed the most: *(check all that apply)*

☐ Brie
☐ Sushi
☐ Gin
☐ Salami
☐ Raw cookie dough

☐ _____

"Trust yourself. You know more than
you think you do." —Benjamin Spock

When did you stop seeing your feet? _____

_____

_____

How many #@!^& strangers touched your belly? _____

Most horrifying birth story you heard: _____

_____

_____

_____

_____

Who was the most annoying couple in your birthing class?

Names: _____

_____

Transgressions: _____

_____

What wacko name did you really want to give the baby?
☐ Ptolemy
☐ Beyoncé
☐ Chattanooga
☐ Quinoa
☐ Bob

☐ _____

HELLO
MY NAME IS
PEPPER   POPPY
MAYA HARPER
ISLA   RUBY

"Smiling babies should actually be categorized by the pharmaceutical industry as a powerful antidepressant." —Jim Gaffigan

Maternity outfit(s) you now loathe: _____

_____

_____

Draw it here:

THINGS YOU DON'T NEED TO HEAR WHEN PREGNANT

HOW MANY HAVE YOU HEARD? CIRCLE THEM!

"DO YOU MISS WINE?"

"ARE YOU SURE IT'S NOT TWINS?"

"ARE YOU WORRIED ABOUT BIRTH DEFECTS?"

"THERE GOES YOUR SEX LIFE."

"YOU SHOULDN'T EAT/DRINK/DO THAT."

"YOU'RE GOING TO HAVE A TOTALLY NATURAL BIRTH, RIGHT?"

"HOW DID YOU CONCEIVE?"

"ARE YOU WORRIED ABOUT BRINGING A LIFE INTO THIS HORRIBLE WORLD?"

"WAS IT PLANNED?"

PLANNER

"ARE YOU CONSTIPATED?"

"ARE YOU WORRIED ABOUT DYING?"

"ISN'T IT DANGEROUS AT YOUR AGE?"

"SHOULD YOU BE WEARING THAT?"

"YOU'RE SO SMALL, ARE YOU SURE THE BABY'S OK?"

"WE WANT YOU TO NAME THE BABY AFTER YOUR FATHER."

"YOU LOOK LIKE AN ELEPHANT SEAL."

"YOU'D BETTER SLEEP NOW."

"MY LABOR LASTED 49 HOURS."

"YOU'RE STILL PREGNANT?"

"WOMEN USED TO JUST DROP THEIR BABIES IN THE FIELDS AND GO ON WORKING."

"LET ME SHOW YOU MY BIRTH VIDEO!"

"YOU'RE CARRYING LOW, IT'S A GIRL."

"YOU'RE CARRYING LOW, IT'S A BOY."

"HOW MUCH HAVE YOUR BOOBS GROWN?"

NO TURNING BACK NOW— BABY'S HERE

LABOR AND DELIVERY

Showtime! Your bags are packed with comfy clothes, nursing bras, your good luck socks, a newborn outfit, and several of the thirty baby blankets you received as gifts. The dog or kids are with a sitter, and you've had your last splurge at a good restaurant.

What were you doing when you went into labor?

_____

_____

How quickly did you demand meds?

_____

_____ gave you drugs and now you worship him/her.

Which birthing techniques proved to be nonsense?

_____

_____

Describe a contraction without using the words "strange," "strong," "excruciating," or "endless":

_____

_____

_____

Okay, you can use those words:

_____

_____

_____

_____

_____

_____

How quickly did you ditch your birth plan? _____

_____

Meanest thing you said to your partner during labor:
- ☐ Stop talking!
- ☐ You did this to me!
- ☐ We're never having sex again!
- ☐ *^$@%!
- ☐ Who says it's your baby!

☐ _____

You stopped caring at all about modesty after _____

_____

When did it hit you that a human being was actually coming out of your body?

_____

What completely ridiculous question did your partner ask the nurse?

_____

_____

_____

Which cartoon character or politician did the baby look like? _____

_____

_____

What did you do when you first held your baby? _____

_____

_____

What did you do with the placenta?
- ☐ Fried it up in a pan
- ☐ Encapsulated it
- ☐ Named it and buried it outside under a full moon
- ☐ Ew
- ☐ What's a placenta?

☐ _____

First thing you wanted to eat: _____

_____

Did you beg or bribe a nurse to come home with you? _____

_____

_____

YOUR BIRTHPLAN, BEFORE AND AFTER

YOU PLANNED FOR:	WHAT REALLY HAPPENED:

EXAMPLES:

Water delivery	"Get me out of this soup!"
No drugs	"Hello anesthesiologist. Are you single?"
Keep my mother away	"I want my mommy!"

GETTING THE HANG OF IT

THE FIRST FEW DAYS OF PARENTING

The hospital sent you home with your baby. Why they thought that was a good idea is beyond your comprehension. You had a properly installed car seat and you could walk, so it appeared you were ready. These first few weeks—when you can measure your baby's age in days—are scary, sweet, funny, and at times, a little like a drug trip.

>>>>>>>>>>>>>>>>>>>>>>> <<<<<<<<<<<<<<<<<<<<<<<<<

Who did you call while freaking out on the first night?

- ☐ Your mother
- ☐ Your mother-in-law
- ☐ The nurses at the hospital
- ☐ The pediatrician
- ☐ Anyone who would take your call

☐ _____

IN CASE OF
EMERGENCY
CALL:
1. MOM
2. DOCTOR
3. THERAPIST
4. EXORCIST

SEARCH

BEAN STUCK IN BABY'S NOSTRIL

The friends and relatives you most wanted to punch were: _____

_____

_____

What completely weird thing happened in the first few days? _____

_____

_____

First time your boy peed on you as soon as you took his diaper off: _____

_____

_____

First time the baby spit up all over you: _____

_____

_____

First time the baby spit up all over you and you didn't really feel compelled
to clean it up:

_____

_____

"'Sleep when your baby sleeps.' Everyone knows this classic tip,
but I say why stop there. Scream when your baby screams. Take
Benadryl when your baby takes Benadryl. And walk around pantless
when your baby walks around pantless." —Tina Fey

DIAPER STINK-O-METER

HEY, THIS ISN'T SO BAD.

WHAT SMELL?

I CAN STILL BREATHE THROUGH MY MOUTH.

WHOA 333

IS IT DOGGIE?

WHEN CAN WE POTTY TRAIN THIS KID?

WHAT DID THIS CHILD EAT?

First apocalyptic poop:

Color: _____

Item(s) of clothing it took out:

Trajectory: _____

_____

Area: _____

_____

First time you were sure you had broken the baby: _____

_____

Second time: _____

_____

Third time: _____

_____

First time you considered calling Child Protective Services on yourself:

_____

_____

_____

The most hideous gift you received was a _____

from _____ .

Which absurdly expensive and useless baby item did you regret buying?

_____

_____

How many copies of *Goodnight Moon* did you get? _____

How many days and nights passed before you realized days and nights were
actually passing?

_____

_____

GOING MOBILE

ROLLING, CRAWLING, STANDING, WALKING, RUNNING, FALLING

Just when you think your baby will never do anything other than lie there and wiggle, the kid rolls over! It's all downhill from there. Next, junior will be crawling, walking, running, and then—boom—borrowing the car.

>>>>>>>>>>>>>>>>>>>>>>>>>>> <<<<<<<<<<<<<<<<<<<<<<<<<<<

What did your kid do later than every other baby, convincing you that something was terribly wrong?

☐ Smile
☐ Crawl
☐ Walk
☐ Talk
☐ Learn algebra

☐ _____

You started wishing the baby would crawl at _____ days/weeks/months.
(circle one)

You started wishing the baby would stay in one place at _____ days/months/weeks.
(circle one)

Baby's first face plant: _____

_____

Baby's first scar or shiner was the result of _____

_____

First time the baby disappeared: _____

_____

What bizarre "crawlesque" form of movement did the baby invent?

_____

"We spend the first twelve months of our children's lives teaching them to walk and talk and the next twelve telling them to sit down and shut up." —Phyllis Diller

Items and furniture the baby pulled down while trying to pull up:

_____

How soon did you stop fretting after falls? _____

_____

Epic childproofing fails: _____

_____

How did baby respond the first time you tried to cram those tiny feet into shoes?

_____

_____

Baby's best hiding place: _____

_____

Describe the baby's goofy toddling walk:

- ☐ Penguin
- ☐ Pigeon
- ☐ Drunk
- ☐ Zombie
- ☐ Drunk zombie

☐ _____

First time the baby bolted in a public place: _____

_____

The baby ninjaed out of the crib at _____ days/months/years.

(circle one)

BABY INJURY CHART

INJURY	DATE	AGE	CAUSE	WHO WAS AT FAULT?

EXAMPLES:

INJURY	DATE	AGE	CAUSE	WHO WAS AT FAULT?
Forehead gash	4/6/17	14 mos	Fell into end table	Dad, who hadn't childproofed it yet
Bloody nose	10/6/17	20 mos	Headbutted mom	Mom, who needs better reflexes

PLEASE TALK! OH MY GOD STOP TALKING!

COMMUNICATION OR LACK THEREOF

You'll spend the first year anxiously waiting to hear your baby's voice and taking bets on the first word. Finally, you'll know the kid's thoughts and needs! Finally, you'll be able to have a conversation! Not so fast: you've still got a year or two of trying to figure out what the baby is saying, cracking up over the crazy stuff that comes out of his mouth, or wishing she'd just be quiet for thirty seconds at a time.

How often did you use the baby as a ventriloquist's dummy? _____

_____

What made the kid laugh the first time? _____

_____

What ridiculous things did you do repeatedly to hear that laugh again?

_____

The baby's first actual, real, genuine word was _____.

> "A two-year-old is kind of like having a
> blender, but you don't have a top for it."
> —Jerry Seinfeld

How long did it take you to figure out what the baby was saying? _____

_____

Words or phrases the baby repeated over and over without rhyme or reason:

_____

_____

When did you first wish the baby would just shut up? _____

_____

_____

Baby's first curse word: _____

_____

$!*#%

Reason for most insane crying fit:

☐ Couldn't reach blankie
☐ Couldn't bite you
☐ Couldn't eat dust bunny
☐ Couldn't fit foot into mouth
☐ Existential crisis

☐ _____

Most appalling thing you thought the kid said (e.g., loudly mispronouncing "truck"):

_____

_____

Most appalling thing you tried to get the baby to say: _____

_____

Most embarrassing public outburst: _____

_____

What just-born animal did the baby's utterances most sound like?

☐ Baby bear
☐ Baby kitten
☐ Baby bird
☐ Baby dolphin
☐ Baby kraken

☐ _____

What odd names did the baby come up with for family members?

_____

Once the kid could talk, you heard "Why?" approximately _____ times a day.

WHAT IS THIS KID SAYING?

KEEP TRACK OF HER SPECIAL
NATIVE LANGUAGE BEFORE IT BECOMES EXTINCT

WHAT THE BABY SAYS	WHAT YOU THINK THE BABY IS SAYING	WHAT THE BABY'S ACTUALLY SAYING

EXAMPLES:

Wafu	I want water, you fool.	Sleep
Row-row	Let's take the boat out	Cheerios

GET ME OUT OF HERE!

LEAVING THE HOUSE

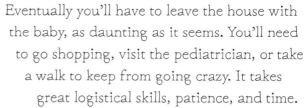

Eventually you'll have to leave the house with the baby, as daunting as it seems. You'll need to go shopping, visit the pediatrician, or take a walk to keep from going crazy. It takes great logistical skills, patience, and time. But you'll get to use all of that baby gear you bought and show off the cute baby outfits that only fit for two weeks.

>>>>>>>>>>>>>>>> <<<<<<<<<<<<<<<<

On the first outing with the baby, who cried?

☐ Baby
☐ You
☐ Both baby and you
☐ Other babies
☐ Strangers

☐ _____

On average, it took _____ days, _____ hours, and _____ minutes to get out of the house with the baby.

First outing that proved to be a really bad idea: _____

_____

Most creative way you changed the baby when there was no changing table or flat surface:

_____

You left a full cart of groceries behind in order to remove your screaming baby from the store _____ times.

Other quick, awkward exits: _____

_____

Which simple things became surprisingly difficult with a baby in tow?

_____

First time there was a diaper blowout and you forgot a change of clothes:

_____

First time this happened and you forgot a change of clothes for yourself:

_____

Most unwelcoming places the baby managed to fall asleep:

_____

You once drove _____ miles before you realized the car seat was unbuckled.

Surprising stuff found in crevices of the car seat and stroller:
(check all that apply)

☐ Cheerios
☐ Pacifiers
☐ Boogers
☐ Cash
☐ Bodily fluids

☐ _____

Restaurants or stores you couldn't go to because something there inexplicably scared the kid:

_____

Things you accomplished in the car while the baby slept in the car seat:

_____

ESCAPE FROM THE HOUSE
A GAME FOR PARENTS WITH TINY BABIES

REALIZE CELL PHONE ISN'T CHARGED, GO BACK 1

FIND CAR CHARGER, GO FORWARD 3

BABY FALLS ASLEEP IN CAR SEAT, GO FORWARD 4

BABY HAS POOP BLOWOUT, GO BACK TO START

FALL ASLEEP STANDING UP, SKIP A TURN

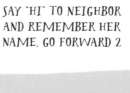

STROLLER NOT IN CAR, GO BACK 1

SAY "HI" TO NEIGHBOR AND REMEMBER HER NAME, GO FORWARD 2

BABY TOSSES SOCK ACROSS THE ROOM, GO BACK 1

START HERE

FORGOT SPARE DIAPERS, GO BACK 1

CAN'T FIND BINKIE, GO BACK 1

BABY FLIPS OUT ABOUT GETTING DRESSED, SKIP A TURN

FIND BINKIE UNDER COUCH, GO FORWARD 2

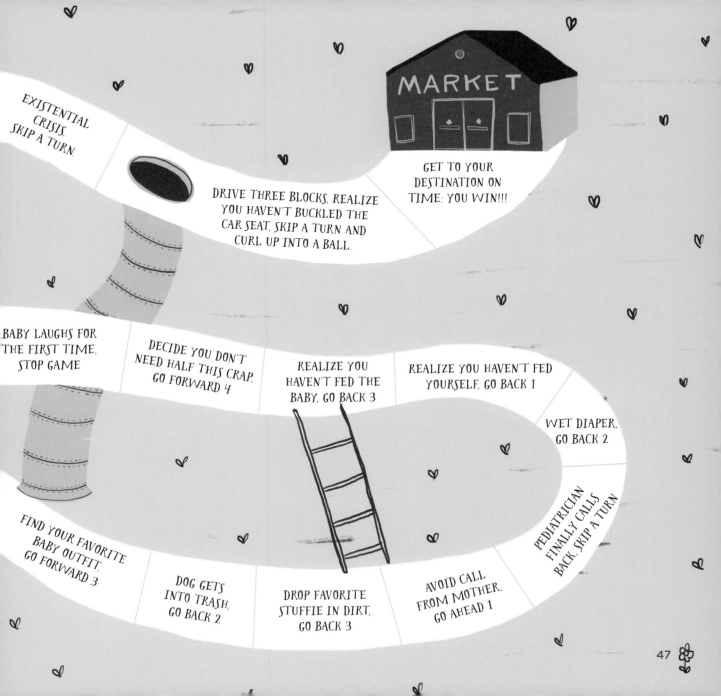

EXISTENTIAL CRISIS, SKIP A TURN.

DRIVE THREE BLOCKS, REALIZE YOU HAVEN'T BUCKLED THE CAR SEAT, SKIP A TURN AND CURL UP INTO A BALL.

MARKET

GET TO YOUR DESTINATION ON TIME: YOU WIN!!!

BABY LAUGHS FOR THE FIRST TIME, STOP GAME

DECIDE YOU DON'T NEED HALF THIS CRAP, GO FORWARD 4

REALIZE YOU HAVEN'T FED THE BABY, GO BACK 3

REALIZE YOU HAVEN'T FED YOURSELF, GO BACK 1

WET DIAPER, GO BACK 2

PEDIATRICIAN FINALLY CALLS BACK, SKIP A TURN

FIND YOUR FAVORITE BABY OUTFIT, GO FORWARD 3

DOG GETS INTO TRASH, GO BACK 2

DROP FAVORITE STUFFIE IN DIRT, GO BACK 3

AVOID CALL FROM MOTHER, GO AHEAD 1

47

FEEDING FRENZY

TRYING TO GET FOOD INTO (OR AT LEAST NEAR) YOUR BABY

Did you ever imagine that you'd spend so much time feeding and thinking about feeding someone else? From nursing to bottles, to baby food, to cutting up hot dogs and pushing peas, much of early parenting is about getting nutrition into one end and dealing with it when it comes out the other. So simple, and yet, so very, very complicated.

Your nursing boobs maxed out at size _____.

Did you or your partner taste the breast milk? ☐ accidentally ☐ on purpose

First experience nursing in public: _____

_____

_____

First time someone judged you for nursing in public or using a bottle:

_____

First time your boobs leaked in public: _____

_____

You inadvertently flashed _____ while nursing.

What did you do to amuse yourself during middle-of-the-night feedings?

_____

_____

Making your own baby food lasted _____ weeks.

Which baby food smelled the most awful?

☐ Peas
☐ Salmon
☐ Chicken and gravy
☐ Meatballs
☐ The two-week-old milk you found in the sippy cup

☐ _____

_____ was the flavor of baby food you secretly enjoyed the most.

Food to blame for the worst stains: _____

_____

Off-limits food that someone fed the baby without your knowledge: _____

_____

Lies you told your child about food: _____

_____

_____

First time the baby ate cat food, dog food, or another food not meant for human consumption:

_____

First time you found food in the kid's hair: _____

_____

How long ago was the meal it belonged to? _____

Non-food items the baby ate: _____

_____

"Even when freshly washed and relieved of all obvious confections, children tend to be sticky."—Fran Lebowitz

BABY'S DISCRIMINATING PALATE: A MATCHING GAME

THE KID'S RESPONSE TO FIRST NIBBLES

FOODS

Rice cereal

Peas

Yogurt

Applesauce

Banana

Cheerios

Avocado

Tofu

Quinoa

Eggs

Chicken

Cheese

Salmon

Blueberries

RESPONSES

Smacked spoon out of your hand

Burst into tears

Stuck up nose

Fed to dog/cat

Cautious interest

Look of utter betrayal

Nom nom nom

Let it dribble back out of mouth

Barf

Happy lip smacking

Grabbed spoon, shoved in mouth

Immediately smeared in hair

Played with it but ingested nothing

Ate first bites happily, then inexplicably refused any more

ONE DAY AT A TIME

ALL THE DAY-TO-DAY STUFF

Parenting is all in the daily details: the good, the bad, the ugly, the sweet, and the very strange.

Insipid picture books you hid: _____

_____

Electronic toys that "got lost": _____

_____

You realized that the parenting books were doing no good and actually making you hate yourself on _____

Creative ways you got the baby to go to sleep:

☐ Driving around in the middle of the night
☐ Getting into the crib with the baby
☐ Reading the *Wall Street Journal* aloud
☐ Xanax
☐ Singing emo tunes

☐ _____

When did you actually start functioning like a human being again, in spite of sleep deprivation?

_____

_____

Celebrity parenting trend you tried: _____

_____

_____ was the scariest thing you fished

out of the baby's mouth.

"When my kids become wild and unruly, I use a nice
safe playpen. When they're finished, I climb out."
—Erma Bombeck

Favorite tiny outfit: _____

How many times was it worn before it was outgrown or ruined? _____

How many miniscule socks did you lose? _____

Which parent cracked first during sleep training? _____

_____

Most unwelcome comment someone made about your choice to stay home
with your baby:

_____

_____

Ninja skills developed to keep from waking a sleeping baby: ———————

——

The baby's comfort talisman was a ————————————————————

The most helpful, and the silliest, parenting tips from others: ————

——

——

——

BABY HURTS YOU BINGO

PULLING HAIR	NIPPLE TROUBLES	INFANT CARRIER-INDUCED BACK PAIN	WHACKING BY BABY IN SWING	TRIPPING OVER BABY GEAR
PULLING CHEST HAIR	KICKING YOU	EX UTERO KIDNEY PUNCH	INFANT CARRIER ELBOW	BREAKING OR SMUDGING GLASSES
HEMORRHOIDS	HEAD BUTTING	GENITAL BASHING	IN UTERO KIDNEY PUNCH	BITING
BOOB GRABBING	STEPPING ON LEGOS	SCRATCHING	SLEEP DEPRIVATION INDUCED INJURY	PROBING FINGERS IN EYES, NOSE, EARS
EARRING PULLING	NURSING-INDUCED NUMB BUTT	LEAPING ONTO SENSITIVE AREAS	FLUIDS IN THE EYE	GRABBING BEARD

BACK TO WORK

KEEP IT PROFESSIONAL.
OR AT LEAST TRY.

All parents work; some just have to dress professionally and appear competent while doing it. We doff our (spit-up stained) hat to all of you, whether you're a full-time working parent, part-time working parent, or stay-at-home parent.

Nastiest comment someone made about your decision to work: _____

_____

You discovered milk / spit-up / pee / poop on your clothes in the middle of a
                        (circle all that apply)

meeting _____ times.

Worst experience nodding off during a meeting: _____

_____

How did you manage to nap at work? _____

_____

_____

You pulled a(n)

☐ binky

☐ diaper (clean)

☐ diaper (dirty)

☐ baby doll

☐ actual baby

☐ _____

out of your bag/briefcase in front of colleagues.

Nursing-related mishaps at work:

☐ Breast pad falling out

☐ Breasts leaking

☐ Kid spitting up all over your outfit during a nursing lunch break

☐ Misplaced milk

☐ Mid-meeting engorgement

☐ _____

Did you ruffle a colleague's hair, kiss the top of his head, or wipe something off his face?

_____

Coworker who most often tried to walk in on you while you were pumping:

_____

"I think God made babies cute so we don't eat them."
—Robin Williams

Baby food you brought for lunch:

_____

Did a colleague add your breast milk to coffee thinking it was cream:
☐ yes   ☐ no   ☐ close call

You forgot your coworker _____'s name
at a critical moment.

Work you did in the middle of the night while nursing your baby:

_____

Times you Skyped into meetings wearing unspeakably stained yoga pants:

_____

When did you realize that your coworkers were less reasonable than your baby?

_____

SHOULD I GO INTO WORK TODAY?

1. Did you get more than three hours of sleep last night? _____
   (2 points for yes, 0 for no)

2. Can you find any clean clothes? _____ (1 point for yes, 0 for no)

3. Did the baby wake more than four times? _____ (0 points for yes,
   2 points for no)

4. Is the tot extra smiley and happy today? _____ (0 points for yes,
   1 point for no)

5. Is the baby teething? _____ (3 points for yes, 1 point for no)

6. Is the baby potty training? _____ (4 points for yes, 1 point for no)

7. Have you recently read a mommy blog telling you that childcare destroys your
   child? _____ (0 points for yes, 2 points for no)

8. Did you read the comments? _____ (0 points for yes, 3 points for no)

9. Will there be good snacks in the break room? _____ (3 points for
   yes, 1 point for no)

10. Do you have any clothes that fit?_____ (2 points for yes, 0 points
    for no)

11. Will staying home give your colleagues an opportunity to snicker about your work ethic? _____ *(0 points for yes, 2 points for no)*

12. Is the weather nice?_____ *(1 point for yes, 2 points for no)*

13. Does your bed look extra inviting? _____ *(0 points for yes, 2 points for no)*

14. Do you have the energy to shower? _____ *(2 points for yes, 0 points for no)*

15. Is your job fun? _____ *(3 points for yes, 0 points for no)*

16. Does the kid smell particularly good today? _____
    (0 points for yes, 3 points for no)

17. Does work pay more than you spend on childcare? _____
    (0 points for no, 4 points for yes)

0-5: Are you crazy?
6-10: Probably not worth it
11-20: How much do you need this job?
21-25: Take some time for an extra cup of coffee
26+: Hurray! Work! Grownups! Responsibility!

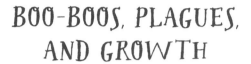

BOO-BOOS, PLAGUES, AND GROWTH

IN SICKNESS AND IN HEALTH

Feeding and changing your baby is your biggest job, but obsessing about the kid's health is a close second. You'll learn an enormous amount about the human body and the curious things that can happen to it. What is that lump? Why is he making that noise? Why won't she poop? Why is he pooping so much? What the hell is that thing? Put the pediatrician on speed dial.

_____ was the scariest baby ailment.

Did the baby pee on the doctor?   ☐ yes   ☐ no

First middle-of-the-night call to the doctor: _____

_____

Describe your experience taking baby's temperature rectally: _____

_____

The kid first barfed on you after _____

_____

First full-family barf fest: _____

After an epic barfing incident, you had to throw away _____

_____

Did you enjoy using the cool tool to suck boogers out of the baby's nose?

_____

Things the baby put up his or her nose that required a visit to the doctor for removal:

☐ Pencil eraser
☐ Peanut
☐ Bean
☐ Cheerio
☐ Lego

☐ _____

First thought when you heard a croupy cough:

☐ My baby is broken
☐ My baby is mortally ill
☐ My baby is barking like a seal
☐ My baby is barking like a dog
☐ My baby is a smoker

☐ _____

Describe your first experience giving the baby medicine: _____

_____

_____

"A child is a curly, dimpled lunatic."—Ralph Waldo Emerson

Favorite method(s) to soothe a colicky or teething baby: _____

_____

_____

Favorite method(s) to soothe a parent with a colicky or teething baby:

_____

_____

Unsolicited diagnoses from nonmedical "experts": _____

_____

_____

UNNECESSARY TRIPS TO THE PEDIATRICIAN

KEEP TRACK, JUST LIKE YOU KEEP TRACK OF
WEIGHT, HEIGHT, AND VACCINATIONS.

DATE	BABY'S AGE	SYMPTOMS	WHAT DID YOU THINK IT WAS?	WHAT WAS IT?

EXAMPLES:

DATE	BABY'S AGE	SYMPTOMS	WHAT DID YOU THINK IT WAS?	WHAT WAS IT?
9/8/16	2 weeks	Weird fingernail	Gangrene	Hangnail
3/11/17	6 months	Lumpy bit on skin	Cancerous growth	Dried baby food

SOCIAL LIFE

FRIENDS AND FRENEMIES

Remember middle school? Sometimes your social life will feel an awful lot like those years. Hold on to those great friends who will take the baby from you and who don't blink when you ask for wine at a playdate. Run from the judgmental, holier-than-thou parents whose rugrats inevitably bite.

>>>>>>>>>>>>>>>>>>>>>>>>>>>>>> <<<<<<<<<<<<<<<<<<<<<<<<<<<<<<<<<<<

What mortifying baby-related thing did you do at a friend's house?

☐ Put a dirty diaper in the recycling bin thinking it was the trash
☐ Called your friend's kid a "little #&@*%"
☐ Sprayed breast milk across the room
☐ Misplaced the baby

☐ _____

Baby friends you didn't like: _____

_____

How did you ditch them? _____

_____

Parents you didn't like: _____

_____

How did you ditch them? _____

_____

Friends you dropped because all they could talk about was their child:

_____

Friends who dropped you because all you could talk about was your child:

_____

Your kid's first screaming fit with a pal was caused by said friend touching

_____

"One thing I had learned from watching chimpanzees with their infants is that having a child should be fun."—Jane Goodall

First time your kid went streaking with a friend: _____

_____

Your go-to friend for parenting advice was: _____

_____

You avoided all advice from: _____

_____

_____ always made the baby cry.

(person)

Whose baby gear was most covetable? _____

_____

Who was the calmest and/or coolest parent friend? _____

It was ☐ reassuring ☐ maddening ☐ _____

Who did you use the baby to avoid? _____

_____

Which friends tried to diagnose your kid with nonsensical ailments?

_____

Most atrocious parenting you witnessed: _____

_____

FIELD GUIDE TO PARENTS TO AVOID
(CHECK OFF EACH AS YOU EXPERIENCE THEM)

ANYONE WHO . . .

- ☐ says she never knew true love until she had her baby

- ☐ responds EVERY SINGLE TIME his child interrupts him

- ☐ has children who can do no wrong

- ☐ devotes every social media post to her baby

- ☐ has a house that's always spotless

- ☐ gets mad at you for scolding his/her child when his/her child is being horrid

- ☐ doesn't think it's funny when you joke about selling your kid on eBay

- ☐ must one-up you in how great (or how lousy) his parenting is

- ☐ gives you parenting advice unless you expressly ask

- ☐ ignores her kid as he beats the crap out of yours

- ☐ calls it "babysitting" when he is taking care of his own child

- ☐ insists your child use hand sanitizer

- ☐ claims her child only likes "adult" food

- ☐ is obsessed with her baby's weight or height or head circumference

PARENTAL TIME

ADULT CONVERSATIONS AND OTHER GROWNUP FUN

For a while, your fantasies will involve nothing but sleep. But eventually you'll remember that your partner is good for more than changing diapers and laughing at your slap-happy poop jokes. Adult conversations, going out, binge-watching, imbibing, sex: you'll enjoy all of these again someday. Maybe even someday soon.

WAAAAHHH...

It took _____ months to rediscover adult activities.

How did your partner woo you back?

☐ Flowers
☐ Home-cooked meal
☐ Massage
☐ A shower
☐ Extra birth control

☐ _____

Code words you developed to talk about sex: _____

_____

Describe the time the kid barged in on you "cuddling": _____

_____

Your explanation for what you and your partner were doing: _____

_____

_____

_____ kept the baby distracted long enough
for a quickie.

How quick was the quickest quickie? _____

_____

The longest conversation you've had that didn't mention the kid was
_____ minutes.

Things that passed for a date:

☐ Walking the dog
☐ Errand-running
☐ 2AM conversation
☐ Sexting during the workday
☐ Baby falling asleep in the car

☐ _____

A "late night out" actually ended at _____ AM / PM

(circle one)

Which "couple time" tip actually worked? _____

_____

Which "couple time" tip made you laugh the hardest? _____

_____

You texted the babysitter _____ times on your first outing.

Highlights of the first blessed overnight trip without children:

☐ Fancy food and drink
☐ Sight-seeing
☐ Sleep
☐ Sex
☐ Peeing alone

☐ _____

"Raising kids is part joy and part guerrilla warfare."
—Ed Asner

EMBARRASSING STORIES

TELL THESE TO HIS PROM DATE
OR SAVE FOR THE TOAST AT HER WEDDING

_____

_____

_____

_____

_____

_____

_____

EXAMPLES:

Baby found by your father-in-law gnawing on an unopened condom package.

Toddler getting stuck butt-down in the toilet.

Kid's habit of requesting a nursing snack by yelling "Boobies!"

CELEBRATE, TRAVEL, AND TAKE EMBARRASSING PHOTOS

HOLIDAYS, TRIPS, AND PARTIES

Holidays and travel with small children seem like such a great idea. And sometimes they are! Things probably won't go as planned, but that can be half the fun. When you hit the road, bring extra diapers, extra snacks, extra cash, and extra patience.

Biggest travel disaster: _____

_____

Your child had a meltdown because you left _____ at home.

The highlight of your trip to _____ was

☐ visiting the children's museum
☐ checking out different toy stores
☐ room service
☐ riding the hotel elevators
☐ spending a night in the hospital

☐ _____

Where was the first travel-related meltdown?

☐ on the plane
☐ at the museum
☐ at an amusement park
☐ at a family function
☐ in the middle of nowhere

☐ _____

HOLIDAYS

How far did you get in your first trick-or-treating effort? _____

_____

What thwarted you?

☐ Child terrified by decorations
☐ Child terrified by someone's costume
☐ Costume malfunction
☐ Overconsumption of candy by child
☐ Overconsumption of candy by adult

☐ _____

That darling "Baby's First Christmas" outfit lasted _____ hours before it was permanently stained.

Difficult lessons learned about babies and holiday decorations: _____

_____

Santa/Easter Bunny photo disasters: _____

_____

_____

_____

On your first New Year's Eve as parents you stayed up until _____ AM / PM

(circle one)

PARTIES

How many people did you invite to the first birthday party? _____

How many of these people were actual children? _____

"You can learn many things from children. How much patience
you have, for instance."—Franklin P. Jones

How did baby's first birthday party end?

☐ Covered in frosting
☐ Covered in tears
☐ Covered in vomit
☐ Covered in kisses
☐ Asleep

☐ _____

Worst child's birthday party experience as host: _____

_____

Worst child's birthday party experience as guest: _____

_____

Describe why you're never invited to _____'s house

ever again: _____

_____

CHART: HALLOWEEN COSTUMES

AGE	DESCRIPTION	HOW LONG DID YOU WORK ON IT?	HOW LONG DID IT STAY ON?

EXAMPLES:

3 months	Grub	3 hours	5 minutes
2	Fire-bellied newt	1 hour	7 hours
3	Batman	Purchased	6 weeks

LITTLE PEOPLE
THE TODDLER YEARS

Are you still filling this out? Do you even remember this book exists? Congrats! Toddlers are sweet, funny, cuddly, and infuriating. There are few things more fun than watching them explore and discover the world. Assuming, fingers crossed, they've had a nap.

First time you audibly laughed at your kid's tantrum: _____

_____

You gave up your plan to ban all TV and computer screens on _____ *(date)*

Weird places the kid hid to poop: _____

_____

First time you threw away the undies rather than deal with the mess: _____

_____

You deeply regretted letting the kid play with the _____

Average number of books and toys you removed from the crib every night:

_____

Which outfit did you have to buy multiples of so that it could be worn for days on end during the _____ phase?

_____

"If you have never been hated by your child,
you have never been a parent."—Bette Davis

First time the tot attempted to pour juice: _____

_____

Weird dreams you had from nodding off while watching children's television:

_____

_____

You stopped checking regularly to see if the sleeping baby was still breathing after _____ years.

Tricks you used to wean the kid off the pacifier: _____

_____

_____

Least favorite toddler exclamation:

☐ "I do it myself!"
☐ "No!"
☐ "Mine!"
☐ "Now!"
☐ "Wake up!"

☐ _____

Inappropriate things your toddler said in public: _____

_____

Longest screaming jag: _____

Most irrational request from your child: _____

_____

THINGS YOU NEVER EXPECTED TO SAY TO ANOTHER HUMAN BEING

EXAMPLES:

"No penises at the dinner table."

"You can't fly!"

"It's only a little bit of poop."